KT-371-450

GLASGOW

GLASGOW

PHOTOGRAPHED BY DOUGLAS CORRANCE
WITH COMMENTARY BY EDWARD BOYD

COLLINS
GLASGOW AND LONDON

To George and Mima

Designed by Derek Porteous

Published by William Collins Sons and Company Limited

Photographs © Scottish Tourist Board
Text © William Collins Sons and Company Limited 1981

First published 1981

Typeset by John Swain and Son Ltd, Glasgow
Printed in Great Britain
ISBN 0 00 435667 5

PREFACE

My great problem with this book has been deciding what to leave out. Glasgow is an amazingly diverse city; the story of its commerce and industry is written in the streets and on the buildings, many of which still proclaim their original usage in beautifully carved frontages; and my respect for the work of Charles Rennie Mackintosh grows the more I discover here of his genius. Glasgow is fortunate in possessing such a masterpiece as the School of Art.

The people are fiercely proud of their city, and I gleaned invaluable information from the most casual of conversations. Their knowledge of its past and their great interest in learning more was a revelation to me.

When recently my father showed me in C. A. Oakley's book *Our Illustrious Forbears* how one of my ancestors had played an important part in the development and prosperity of the city, I felt an immediate affinity which I hope makes me less of an outsider.

If this book adds in any way to someone's view of the city, its purpose will have been achieved.

DOUGLAS CORRANCE

INTRODUCTION

It is always important when discussing a theory, a personality, an event, or even merely voicing an opinion, to be prepared to answer the wry challenge: "Who are you and where are you from?" Essentially this is a demand for credentials with an underlying sardonic suggestion that you could be, and possibly are, talking nonsense. With this in mind, therefore, let me clear some ground.

The small town where I was born is on the Ayrshire coast and about thirty miles from Glasgow which brings it within a kind of quasi-planetary relationship with the city. Nowadays thirty miles is nothing, the internal combustion engine having reduced it to the equivalent of a short stroll; but in those days thirty miles was thirty miles and, psychologically, sometimes even more. I can recall not so very elderly people who had never been to Glasgow and who regarded it as a way station through which an astonishing number of relatives had had to pass on the way to America or Canada. However, if Mahomet was not prepared to go to the mountain, the mountain was more than prepared to go to Mahomet, especially during the two weeks in July known as the Glasgow Fair Fortnight which involved a rigid social ritual. Phase One of this began almost as soon as the rigours of the Scottish New Year had been undergone and survived. Then you got the first intimations that the ritual was under way from the women talking in the shops or chatting across the garden fence, the key question being: "Are ye haein' ony saut watter folk this year?" I thought, and still think, that "saut watter folk" is one of the most beautiful phrases I have ever heard. I wrote, years later, a radio play of which I cannot remember the plot or even one single line for the sheer joy of its title "Saut Watter Folk". Fortunately the BBC took the title in its Olympian stride which was just as well. "Salt Water People" may be the English equivalent but you don't have to be an ultra-Nationalist to see that it isn't the same thing at all.

The second phase was recognizably under way when a rash of mini-posters appeared in every street-facing window; and here I have a shameful confession to make. My grandmother, who was regarded as being infallible in everything else, had certain blind spots, one of which was to regard me as an intellectual. In practice this meant that anything regarding the written word was referred to me. I am baffled as to how this misconception arose or what I ever did to foster it, but it was never challenged for the simple reason that nothing my grandmother ever decreed was ever challenged. So it came about that, willy-nilly, I was elected as PR Man – at the age of eleven or thereabouts – for the fact that my grandmother was prepared to let her front room with its two recessed beds to anyone from

Glasgow who looked respectable and who survived her probing questioning which usually boiled down to answering yes or no to the simple demand, "Are you a Catholic?" Thus briefed, I set to work with a piece of cardboard and a scratchy pen and in due course produced something for her to stick in the window which she did without looking at it, such was her trust in my intellectuality. Judge of our surprise when, a short time later, we looked out of the window to see a queue formed, most of whom were giggling and guffawing and pointing the finger of scorn. My grandmother went tearing outside, jostled her way to the front of the throng and read what I had inscribed: "Room to let", and beneath that "12 beds". It took me years to live that down if, indeed, I have lived it down. A simple moment of inattention, a careless lapse, and my credibility was gone for ever. An older cousin took over the chore which soon became a sinecure since my grandmother never attempted to let her front room again.

The week before the Saut Watter Folk arrived was frenetic. Everywhere there was polishing and scrubbing. Some hypocrites even went so far as to paint the walls of the rooms that were to be occupied by the invading Glaswegians. Others justified not doing anything by saying that the arriving hordes would be put in a condition of shock if confronted by excessive cleanliness, not being used to such a phenomenon. Rosters were worked out, setting forth what children should sleep in whatever beds were available and which should spend the summer hours of darkness on makeshift arrangements on the floor. There was great competition for the latter to the extent that those who, by some luck of the draw or miscalculation by their parents, spent the whole fortnight in a warm comfortable bed, felt cheated and deprived. Thus the days wore on till the day of days – the Coming of the Saut Watter Folk.

Everyone was up early that July morning. Indeed, it is debatable if anyone genuinely slept the night before. Breakfasts were minimal and were bolted down; and an hour before the first train was due in, every male under the age of fourteen was hurrying barefoot down the cobbled street that led to the station. The main endeavour was to secure a vantage point on the bridge that straddled the railway when the level crossing gates were closed. Once that was achieved nothing remained but to wait. There were, of course, endless false alarms before the train arrived; but eventually arrive it did and we cheered it as though it had come to raise a siege.

I swear that the coaches of that train were elasticated. Years later when I saw that famous scene in a Marx Brothers film where people keep cramming into a cabin beyond all logic of space the first thing that occurred to me was "Glasgow Fair in reverse". I remembered bodies spilling out of a train, the men in incongruous serge suits and white sandshoes, the women in floral dresses, the children dressed up to extinction. There were cheap fibre suitcases and shopping bags that clinked suspiciously. They poured out of the station in a flood of cheerfulness and by the time they reached the Cross, about half a mile away, you would have sworn that only the women and children had come on holiday, the men having been swallowed up by the various public houses en route.

For the next fortnight they took over the town. They beat us homerically in football matches that lasted all day. They all swam like fishes while we, born and brought up on the coast, floundered around like harpooned whales. The local fish-and-chip shops did a land-office business. The girls brought a sophistication that set the local standards until their return the following Fair. All of them spoke a strange language filled with an urban, alluvial poetry, a language which we imitated but failed singularly to reproduce. When they returned home in their elasticated trains, a strange silence fell, a sense of loss. They had given us our town back and we did not quite know what to do with it. Something had gone out of it literally and metaphorically.

A war later, I set off on what I did not know then was a personal odyssey. As the song says, "I been in some big towns; I heard me some big talk . . ." I was in Paris when John F. Kennedy was shot. I was in London when the Sixties were turning the world upside down and a Glasgow boy was king of Carnaby Street. I was in Manchester which I liked, I realize now, because it reminded me of Glasgow. Finally I came back to the most generous, unexpected, long-suffering, infuriating, gutsy city I know. I have been described as a Glasgow writer (never by a Glaswegian) but I know this not to be the case. There are always nuances that someone born in Ayrshire is going to miss. Both my daughters, however, were born in Glasgow. I have a feeling that they may succeed where I have failed.

EDWARD BOYD

If love is blind, as we are continually assured it is, then Glasgow's artists must surely have loved their city. Sadly, they have never given any convincing proof of having been able to see it. It is true that, for about three decades at the turn of the century, there was a group of painters who are now known as the Glasgow School; but they seem to have been preoccupied with profitable portraits, rural landscapes and oriental whimsy. Contemporary artists turn an equally blind eye. Meanwhile, the morning mist rises from the river, cranes rest as redundant as dinosaurs, and James McNeill Whistler, looking down from Heaven, shakes his head in disbelief at a thousand lost opportunities.

11

On the skyline the twentieth century
proclaims itself. The language is
everywhere in general and nowhere in
particular; but the accent is universally
high-rise. Arthur Koestler has coined the
perfect phrase for it: Esperanto
achitecture. In the foreground the older
buildings rescue the eye and the mind
from the sheer banality of the New
Barbarism. Traffic streams across the
Victoria Bridge better known to
Glaswegians as the Stockwell Street Brig.
The clipper *Carrick*, now transformed
into the R.N.V.R. Club, sits brooding on
her own reflection. Will she ever sail the
seven seas again? Or has she become a
ship in a bottleneck?

Every city is a continuing mystery. Why is such and such a street called by the name it bears? Why is the West End always more up-market than the East End? Who was Alexander Kirkland whose architectural credits include the lovely Suspension Bridge that spans the river from Clyde Street to Carlton Place? Was he an architect at all or, as has been suggested, a brilliant entrepreneur who manipulated other men's greater talents? Whatever the answer, he took it with him to America where he became Commissioner of Public Buildings in Chicago. Behind him he left this little corner of Glasgow with its faint echo of music from a *bal musette*.

As early as 1556 the inhabitants of Glasgow, Renfrew and Dumbarton "wrought for six weeks at a time removing a ford at Dumbuck and some sand banks, which enabled small craft to reach the Broomielaw". In 1812, when Henry Bell's forty-foot steamship *Comet* grounded on a shoal near Renfrew, the gentlemen aboard stepped over the side and pushed her clear. By the outbreak of World War One the Clyde, deepened and dredged, was launching one third of the world's steamships. Now the sun setting over the silent river and the still cranes have become a comment, a melancholy metaphor.

The little ships of the Clyde have not all been equally fortunate in finding a chronicler. The Clyde puffers have perhaps fared best of all thanks to a combination of the late Neil Munro and television. The Clyde pleasure steamers, though extinct as the dodo for all practical purposes, survive as the dynamic of a flourishing literary industry based on the golden summers of yesteryear. Yet no writer has come forward to champion the dredging hoppers (known ironically as "The Skye Navy") or to celebrate the tugs that fussed among the great liners, bantam mercenaries protecting blind emperors.

A cryptic notice in a Govan shipyard sets the mind seething with questions. What is a Teabagger? In what respects does a Teabagger differ from, say, a Carpetbagger? Isn't there something fundamentalist about that phrase "burning pit"? Could Teabaggers be some fanatical religious secret society plotting to take over the universe?

Another fascinating point is the name beneath the warning notice: are we intended to believe in the existence of someone called Hugh Dunnett? Can it be mere coincidence that if you say the name quickly enough or without your dentures it sounds like "whodunnit"? Or, even more alarming, "youdunnit".

The smiling gentleman on the right could only tell us that he wasn't Hugh Dunnett.

Nowadays we are suspicious, even fearful, of technology to an extent that would have had the Victorians sniffing in contempt. The nineteenth century embraced technology as an ally that would bring the world of nature to heel. The present century views it as something that might bring the world of nature to a sudden and unpleasant end. The Victorian imagination would have found no difficulty in visualizing the welder above as a logical descendant of one of the knights from Agincourt or Bannockburn. Our more pessimistic contemporary imagination would be more likely to equate him with some sinister figure from *Star Wars* or *The Empire Strikes Back.*

Ships moored at Meadowside Quay suggest that world shipping has not entirely abandoned the Clyde. The fact remains, nevertheless, that the great days have gone. Those who believe that the Clyde made Glasgow lament a vanished glory. Those who maintain that Glasgow made the Clyde see no cause for despair. Even the drop in the city's population from 1,300,000 in 1941 to something under 800,000 forty years later they view unperturbed. Today's eco-philosophers tell them that Small is Beautiful and that any city with more than half a million inhabitants is ungovernable. And what about those reports that Saint Mungo's salmon are cautiously returning to the Clyde?

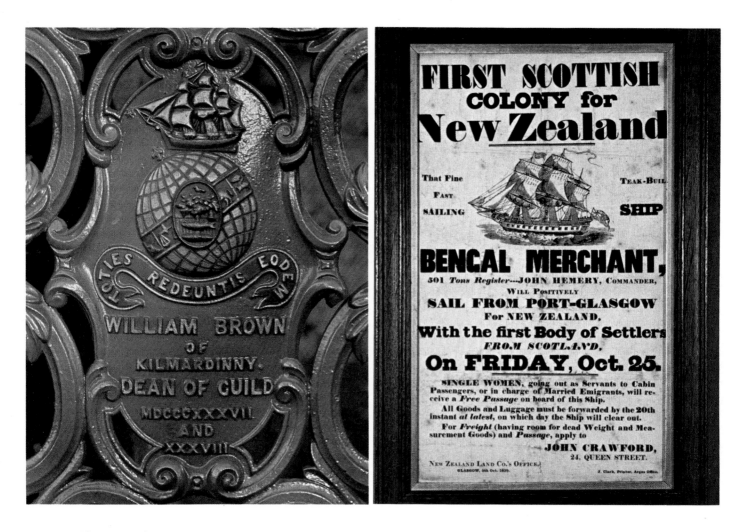

The crest on the gates of the Necropolis is that of the Merchant Guild who owned the site east of the Cathedral. In 1831, Dr John Strang suggested that "a garden cemetery and monumental decoration" would be beneficial to public morals and the improvement of manners. Afire with reforming zeal, the City Fathers bought the site and immediately raised a monument to John Knox on its highest point. By 1857 the Necropolis was described as "the hallowed depository of the ashes of our most distinguished citizens". The first person buried there was Joseph Levi, a Jewish quill merchant who died of cholera. The poster, which speaks for itself, is in the People's Palace.

Crossing the Clyde was, for a long time, a simple and traditional business – a man rowed you across in a boat. Even in 1858 when the Clyde Navigation Trust was empowered to provide ferry services, it could not see beyond old-fashioned muscle power. Looking back, it seems remarkable that midway through that astonishing century which raised Glasgow to a peak when the city was practically the workshop of the world no one appeared to have noticed that a proletariat had emerged whose transport requirements demanded a new, and larger, sophistication. The point was made tragically on 6th April 1861 when the overcrowded Govan Ferry capsized, drowning seven passengers. The official reaction appears to have been simply to regard this as a capricious and isolated Act of God. No lesson was learned, no conclusion drawn. Then, about six o'clock in the evening of St Andrew's Day 1864, twenty-seven workmen crushed aboard the Finnieston Ferry. The water was very choppy and the overcrowding made steering well-nigh impossible. The ferry was beam on to the opposite shore when the *Inveraray Castle* sailed past. The wash of her passing caught the ferry boat and poured inboard. The workmen panicked towards the lee side and the ferry boat turned over. Of the twenty-seven passengers only eight survived. This time the point got home, having cost only twenty-six lives. In 1865 steam ferries made their appearance and by 1900 there were vehicular ferries at Finnieston, Whiteinch and Govan, with passenger ferries at intervals from York Street to Meadowside.

Now the steam ferries that replaced the rowing boats have themselves been superseded. They exist only in an affectionate but vanishing folklore. Speeding over the new motorway bridges you are too concerned with watching the maniac behind in your driving mirror to have time for anything else. On the old Govan Ferry you had time to reflect that you were travelling sedately along a historical path, one of the oldest-established crossing places on the Clyde.

The Kingston Bridge is Glasgow's latest
and its thirteenth. The superstitious might
say it shows. The sceptics would say
random accidents and reckless driving
play a bigger part than any quirk of fate.

Bruce and Hay who designed the
Co-operative Wholesale Society's
building in 1897 were accused of re-using
the design which won second place in the
City Chambers competition. Naturally
they denied this and who are we to
disbelieve them after all this time.

Motorway construction does not always destroy the environment. The Mitchell Library now has a shrub-lined forecourt for its earnest schoolchildren, students, old men, and sundry other seekers after knowledge within its splendidly ornate interior. In this off-hand age do they also find the library staff amazingly willing to help with the search for the most arcane truth?

The nineteenth-century tobacco baron, Stephen Mitchell, left Glasgow the money for a large public library. This is its third and permanent home, built in 1911.

Queen Street Station is one end of the polarity between Glasgow and Edinburgh. From here the trains leave to take Glaswegians into exile in the capital city; and here it should be explained that rabid Glaswegians regard any period exceeding twenty-four hours spent in Edinburgh as exile. The station was built on part of what was originally the Cow Loan along which cattle were driven by two herds appointed by the magistrates. These herds had to swear an oath of loyalty and had to post guarantees "for loyal and true administration in their office". Passengers who feel they are being treated like cattle should remember this.

A lot can be inferred about the character and nature of a city's inhabitants by watching how they queue. In London people queue inside an invisible capsule of defensive space. They stand like seagulls who always leave enough room between each other to guarantee an unimpeded take-off. This would seem to indicate a profound distrust of one's fellow men. Glasgow people queue in tribal fashion. This may indicate gregariousness or it may simply be a reaction to Glasgow's weather, a huddling together for mutual warmth. The conversation will invariably revolve round the eternal mystery: why Glasgow buses either do not turn up at all or else suddenly appear in motorcades.

When the Central Station Bridge was built in 1866 it created a tunnel where it crossed Argyle Street and unwittingly brought into being one of the most famous meeting-places in Glasgow. It became a rendezvous for the Highlanders who had flooded into the city, and some smug, superior Lowlander dubbed it "The Hielanman's Umbrella". At one time you could stand there for hours without hearing the English language. Visiting Sassenachs will tell you that the same holds good today, and all over the city.

The taxi in the foreground has a certain accidental rightness. Its ancestors – the sedan chairs of the eighteenth century – were largely carried by Highlanders.

Writers on the architecture of Glasgow tend to be a bit sniffy about the former entrance to the St Enoch subway. Two of them, indeed, have written it off in an authoritative tome as "absurdly insignificant". Yet this so-called absurdity gives it an endearing charm. It evokes cuckoo clocks carved in the Black Forest or those little wooden toys that had a little carved lady emerge from a little carved cottage when the day was going to be wet. The fact that the little carved man only came out when the forecast was fine probably touched a chord in the Glasgow man's machismo.

The merchants of Victorian Glasgow
pushed the city up the success ladder until
it was the Second City of the British
Empire. Presbyterian to the backbone,
they paid lip service to the biblical
injunction about God and Mammon. In
practice they raised temples to Mammon
all through the city. The beautiful Ca
d'Oro building in Gordon Street is one of
them. It was designed by John Honeyman
as a furniture warehouse. A later addition
to the building, the mansard attic, does its
best to destroy the Ca d'Oro's splendid
saliency. The effect is that of seeing the
Doge of Venice in a cloth cap.

Policemen and taxis, according to the folk wisdom, are never there when they are wanted. This hoary old gripe has, no doubt, been aired yet again by the above ladies-in-waiting, their partners and their progeny. Then the more particular gripes take over. "Been waiting here longer than it took me to come from London (or Manchester or Birmingham or Liverpool)". The taxi rank at the Central Station Hotel has seen and heard it all before.

A practical tip from a taxi-driver: "Check there isn't a football match on. When Rangers play Celtic, some of us taxi-drivers tend to give the Central Station rank a body swerve."

Our tidy minds prefer things in their tidy, proper place. When they are not, the normal is disrupted and the way is open for the abnormal or even the paranormal or those things that lurk deep in the subconscious. People like Alfred Hitchcock and the surrealist painter Magritte understood this. The man above should be walking up the eighteenth fairway at St Andrews. His attitude is right as are the dangling cigarette and the golf club. Even the coat and the navy blue and yellow trainers could be amiable eccentricities.

What's he doing walking past the oldest building in Glasgow with his golf club and trainers? What would happen if . . .? Is that door opening slowly . . .?

Is it heresy to suggest that "Wee Willie Winkie" might not be a nursery jingle but rather a satire on the "promulgators" who prowled the Saturday streets of eighteenth-century Glasgow, imposing their ten o'clock Calvinist curfew?

> Wee Willie Winkie
> Rins through the toon;
> Upstairs an' doonstairs
> In his nicht goon;
> Chappin' at the windae
> Tirlin' at the lock:
> Are a' the bairnies in their beds?
> It's past ten o'clock.

A stark description of how the bigots operated. And Wee Willie Winkie is an inspired name for a pious, canting hypocrite. And one certain way of defusing uncomfortable satire is to sidetrack it into Children's Corner. Like Gulliver's Travels. The man who might have told us is buried in the Necropolis across from Glasgow Cathedral.

When St Paul wrote about "sounding brass" he coined a near-perfect phrase. There is something about brass, a militant stridency, a don't-try-to-ignore-me quality which makes it the ideal medium for heliographing to the world who you are and what you have to offer. The operative word here is "heliographing". Our old flight sergeant, Button Stick Bill, would have had a few well-chosen and highly profane words to say to some of the firms above. His simple precept: "If you can't beat the enemy, you can always dazzle him".

In the doorway, the City Chambers ponder this reflectively.

George Square can be regarded as an example of the Glasgow preparedness to forgive and forget. It was originally christened in honour of George the Third who, as every schoolboy used to know, lost his American colonies by his sheer ineptitude and in so doing destroyed Glasgow's flourishing and lucrative tobacco trade. Forgiveness was far from total, however, or perhaps there was some lingering, secret Jacobite influence at work in the city. When it was proposed to put a statue of the mad Hanoverian king on top of a column in the centre of the square, someone sabotaged the proposal and Sir Walter Scott ended up there instead.

The editor of a now defunct Glasgow
newspaper once wrote a book about
Glasgow in which he voiced certain
qualms about the City Chambers. "The
sense of wealth about the place is too
insistent", he complained. This prim
assessment shows a sad misconception of
the Glasgow character. When a
Glaswegian has money he doesn't care
who knows it or who helps him to spend
it. So why should he deny the same
privilege to his elected representatives?
Certainly the above senior citizens do not
appear to be dreaming dark egalitarian
dreams of the day when Scottish Cossacks
will stable their horses in the marble halls.

The Tron Kirk, on the south side of the
Trongate, has weathered fire and storm,
vandals, and being downgraded into a
storehouse. Now, in yet another
transformation, it has just become a
theatre. Situated close to what was once
the mercantile centre of Glasgow, it has
seen the primitive accumulation of the
early shopkeepers explode into the gaudy
efflorescence of the Tobacco Lords then
sag back into more mundane
money-making. It has seen royal
processions and weavers' riots. It has
watched Bailie Nicol Jarvie become
Dickson McCunn and Dickson McCunn
become multi-national. What else was left
but to become a theatre?

Nature imitates art in Argyle Street. The statue might represent one of Prince Charlie's Highlanders who got left behind when the Prince's army moved out in low dudgeon. His name is something like Angus Gog or perhaps Hamish Magog. He bows his head in shame at being reduced to wearing a dish-cloth in place of a sporran.

For the man in the doorway, the Forty-five Rebellion is yesterday's hassle. He has strictly contemporary problems and as he mulls them over in his mind he has the vaguely brooding aspect of an umpire whose cricket match has just disappeared before his very eyes.

No man is an island; but a boy and a girl – sometimes. A young couple in the Buchanan Street pedestrian precinct evoke old tunes from long-gone Hollywood musicals: "Isn't It A Lovely Day To Be Caught In The Rain?", "A Bench In The Park", "Under My Umbrella". She likes him because she thinks he looks like Jimmy Connors, the American tennis ace. He likes her because he thinks that *she* looks like the American tennis ace, Jimmy Connors. He is absolutely convinced that this time it's The Real Thing. Otherwise why would he put up with her letting the rain run off the umbrella down his neck?

North Italian Gothic is how architects pigeonhole the Stock Exchange seen here in an unusual perspective which turns it into a decorative stone arrowhead flying along the west side of Buchanan Street towards the fashionable church of St George's Tron. The Stock Exchange was first mooted in 1844 during the euphoric days of the railway boom and was completed in that year of revolutions, 1848. St George's Tron is older by about half a century. The four obelisks were originally intended to be statues of the four Evangelists, Matthew, Mark, Luke and John.

The layout of this trio for brass accidently forms itself into an intelligence test. You know the kind of thing: which of these words/objects/whatever is the odd man out? The answer in this case is obviously the centre picture which shows the letter box of the General Post Office in George Square. This was hotly disputed by an eight-year-old to whom we showed the pictures and posed the question. She insisted that the correct answer, the real odd man out, was the brass plate identifying Hunter Barr and Co. The reason? "The other two are *clean*".

The Mitchell Library now incorporates an excellent small theatre not the least of whose fascinations is the enigmatic group of statuary on its façade. A divinity student is convinced that the figures represent Macbeth's three witches following a visit to Denmark for a sex change operation. A well-known Scottish actress was equally convinced that the figures were actors whom a certain director who shall be nameless had driven up the wall. A chappie from the Scottish Arts Council stared at the group through a monocle for a few minutes then asked what was the hidden symbolism of the fellow standing up with a sawn-off elephant's foot on his head?

There was this firm that decided, one day, that their business premises needed a facelift. The first item on their list of improvements, they decided, was to be a new glass door. They telephoned and ordered one. The man said fine and promised to take care of the business over the weekend. When the staff arrived for work on Monday morning they were confronted with the door above. Behind it lay a discarded battery from a hearing aid.

The picture on the right shows a detail of the Royal Scottish Academy of Music and Drama reflected in a window of St George's Tron church.

Tobacconists in Glasgow remain viable in an era of cloned supermarkets. The reason may simply be that it is that kind of era. A certain middle-class snobbery also operates in their favour. The owner is as bourgeois as his clients. He wears the same school tie, the same conservative suits. He is perhaps the third, or even fourth, generation in the business. He may even benefit from a race memory of the Tobacco Lords.

His staff is female, neat, dowdy, not young. They have the slightly daunting kindliness of royal nannies. Their perfect customer is pipe-smoking, tweedy, and was probably written by John Buchan.

In the days when successful merchants
still managed to combine a sense of
locality with a civic conscience (it was in
1791 to be precise) a Tobacco Lord named
Walter Stirling left a thousand pounds,
certain property and his collection of 804
books for the founding of what was to be
the first public library in Glasgow. Initially
the project was housed in a room in the
Surgeon's Hall, George Square. Later it
was moved to 48 Miller Street and finally
came to rest in the Royal Exchange
Building which incorporates what was
once the town house of another famous
Tobacco Lord, William Cunninghame.
Does that make a case for the "No
Smoking" regulation to be waived in this
particular library?

Visitors to Glasgow, especially tourists
from overseas, are almost invariably loud
in their praises of the men and women –
especially women – who serve in the city's
shops and stores. Indeed their patience,
courtesy, tact and good humour are in
grave danger of becoming proverbial.
This may, in part, be an over-reaction by
people who arrive in Glasgow with very
low expectations, the media having
conditioned them to expect a
murder-a-minute hell set in a landscape of
total urban destruction. Yet the praise of
the shop assistants is more than simply a
disguised sigh of relief. When one
remembers London shop assistants
whose attitudes vary within the narrow
limits of pseudo-aristocratic disdain and
plain old-fashioned Anglo-Saxon
boorishness, the people behind
Glasgow's shop counters become
paragons indeed.

This has its own contradictions. The
touchy independence of the Glaswegian
temperament ought, by all predictions, to
clash violently with the basic requirement
of salesmanship which is, after all, to
defer. The Glasgow way out of this
paradox is to abolish all ideas of deferring
in favour of sharing an experience. You
need a new hat for the Tory Party
Conference? All right, let's you and I get
together and choose one; and when we've
reached agreement about the one we
want, just give me the money and I'll see it
gets to the right person. The experience is
the same whether you are shopping
around for matching pink pearls or
selecting a Christmas gift from the
Aladdin's caves that Glasgow's big stores
transform themselves into at that time of
the year. To call it a technique is
superficial and insulting to both parties
involved. It is a meeting of two
independences which ends with neither
one feeling manipulated, threatened or
undermined.

In a consumer society, people consume
things at different rates; and something
that may be discarded as clapped out by A
may appeal to B as still having a certain
useful life expectancy. Shops like the one
above make use of this differential. It is to
be found near the Barrows, the famous
open-air market which is to Glasgow what
their Flea Markets are to Amsterdam and
Paris.

Mad buyers do not necessarily depend
on mad customers but it helps. The man
with the clock may not have been mad
when he went into the shop but he is
getting madder by the minute. He has only
just come out of the place and already he
has been asked twice if he wouldn't have
been better off with a wrist watch.

A professor can research through an ancient midden and become respected as an archaeologist. A man down on his luck does it and is despised as what is known in Glasgow parlance as a "midgieraker", which may be defined as "one who searches dustbins and middens for anything he can eat, wear, sell or otherwise dispose of". The current and apparently insatiable demand for antiques could be seen as a kind of up-market midgieraking. Things that our grandparents threw out have been redeemed, polished up and given a new lease of life as the basis of a fashionable and flourishing industry.

As long as there remains the slightest vestige of rugged individualism there will be a small shop on the corner, an enterprise run by one man or woman. Increasingly, however, the species is becoming endangered. Indeed, at a time when even the moneyed multiples are screaming out in pain because of higher rating, the very existence of the wee shop savours of the miraculous. Yet they continue to spring up like mushrooms even if they tend to vanish equally quickly. Perhaps they represent some tiny parable of the human spirit: or perhaps, like second marriages, they represent the triumph of hope over experience.

When our cave ancestors ran out of wall space on which to inscribe their matchless graffiti, they turned to each other and started to produce illustrated men. Thousands of years later this vernacular art form is still with us. The tattooist in the Gallowgate can fix you up with anything from a tiny swallow at the base of your thumb to a full-scale opus that turns its wearer into a kind of walking mural. Tattooists generally flourish in time of war but dedicated practitioners fear a falling off of standards in the event of World War Three. After all, what kind of satisfactory job can you do in four minutes?

Behind this picture lies the story of the strange cure of a celebrated Glasgow alcoholic. His wife had tried threats, appeals, aversion therapy, the lot, all to no avail. Then someone told her that on the counter of the bar he frequented was a plaster statuette of two dogs advertising a famous brand of Scotch. The idea was born. She tethered two borrowed terriers outside the little shop where he bought his papers. One morning, feeling no pain, he went to the shop and saw the dogs. He turned pale. When his wife insisted she could see nothing he turned even paler. Since then he has become a thoroughly unpleasant teetotaller and his wife wishes she had left well alone.

A moment of truth at the Barrows, famous Glasgow al fresco market. To buy or not to buy, that is the question, and it is repeated on countless occasions every Saturday and Sunday when the market is open. The well-off also visit the place, not so much in search of bargains but because they have become addicts of the place and its atmosphere and its people. Perpetual optimists come in quest of that grimy old painting that will turn out to be a Vermeer and shatter world records at Sotheby's. And comedians, suitably disguised, come to steal the best gags from the salesmen's patter.

In 1778 an embryonic police force was set up in Glasgow only to be disbanded three years later when the citizens refused to be assessed for the upkeep of the guardians. An Act of Parliament by the London government refused to accept stinginess as a valid reason for the city not being policed, and in 1800 the Glasgow Police made their entrance onto the city scene.

The policewomen above find their life varied and exciting. Yesterday they were part of a police presence at an anti-nuclear demonstration in a Glasgow park. Today they find themselves at the Highland Games in Scotstoun, counting calories.

Still life with strawberry tarts; but no
evocations of Wimbledon, high summer
and men sitting atop stepladders arguing
with brown-legged international
petulants. Glaswegians play tennis –
between showers of rain; cricket within
the same meteorological limitations; but
this macho city, as far as sport is
concerned, sees summer negatively as
that time of year that is a hiatus to be
endured between the end of one football
season and the start of another. A passion
for strawberry tarts, therefore, is a pure
emotion, unsullied by extraneous
associations and completely unaffected by
the moans of dieticians who are aghast at
the Glaswegian's notoriously sweet tooth
and generally deplorable eating habits.

The first thing that would strike an expatriate Glaswegian returning to his native city after a twenty-year absence would be the number of restaurants now competing for his custom. It is possible to do a gastronomic world tour within the city's bounds, and if Tibetan restaurants are still thin on the ground, you could always go to a Chinese restaurant and pretend you are in Lhasa by asking them to put rancid butter in your tea.

Despite the proliferation of new places offering their exotic ethnic fare, some of the older established restaurants still soldier on, dedicated to the belief that home-produced victuals rank with the best the world can offer. This one is in Exchange Place.

The fishmonger in the High Street could throw no light on the presence in the Old Fish Market of a pair of battered and rather weather-beaten statues. One of them was obviously Shakespeare but who was the other? A mermaid, he suggested, neatly beheading a cod, but the lady's sturdy stone legs made this unlikely. The chance reading of a letter in a local newspaper solved the mystery. The statues originally graced the façade of the Citizens Theatre and were placed here for storage. A statue of Robert Burns which originally accompanied them was transferred to the new theatre in the Tron Kirk for an undisclosed fee. Shakespeare has now joined him.

Darby and Joan, tripe and onions, Bonnie and Clyde, Hobbs and Sutcliffe, sausage and mash, all represent immortal and demotic partnerships. Right up there with them is the happy and harmonious alliance of fish and chips, the joyful pabulum of generations of Glasgow punters. People who know about such things have said that the nutritive value of this democratic dish is remarkably high, which any Glaswegian could have told them all the time. Glasgow gourmets insist that fish and chips should be first flooded with vinegar before being eaten out of the paper with the fingers, preferably while walking along the pavement so that their unbeatable bouquet is available to anyone who cares to share it.

Lunch time in George Square, the city centre. Half-time in the serious game of earning a living. A lull in which to find out whether the fast food merchants have done their best – or worst. Talk about that television show last night or tomorrow's disco prospects (I'm staying in tonight to wash my hair). In the background the bus to Baghdad, until you look closer.

Elsewhere, in the fruit shop a girl opts for vitamin C and doesn't care who knows it. Had she been around in the time of good King Charles, Nell Gwynn might have wound up at Drury Lane pleading for her old job back.

Glasgow has this in common with New York: both cities became immigrant targets, the difference being merely one of scale. The starvation years of the Irish Famine brought unprecedented numbers of Irishmen across the Irish Sea (one ship, the *Londonderry*, arrived in 1848 with 72 suffocated corpses in its hold). Russian and Polish pogroms contributed their quota of Jews. Later came the Lithuanians, some of them arriving with luggage labels round their necks, human merchandise addressed to this or that colliery or foundry. The most recent arrivals are from much farther afield.

53

One of the more permanent results of Moody and Sankey's evangelism towards the end of the nineteenth century was the Tent Hall in Steel Street off the Saltmarket. This was originally, as the name suggests, a tent, the Evangelical Tent, on Glasgow Green, and such was its success that something larger and more permanent soon became necessary. The Glasgow United Evangelistic Association then built the present building, retaining the name as a reminder of its origin. Its centenary was celebrated in 1975. Free Sunday breakfasts were served to those who needed them, a practice that lasted from 1875 unbroken until they were discontinued in 1979. The Tent Hall is now owned by the YMCA.

Anyone looking for the perfect urban symbol need look no further than the people who sell its newspapers. They are as urban as sparrows and as local as a street name. If Dickens were to rewrite *Bleak House* with a contemporary setting and latter-day characters then Little Jo the crossing sweeper would surely be a newsboy and not a passive wet. We recall, from our earliest schoolbook, someone called Paper Nellie. She wore a red tammy and went around in her bare feet even when the snow was thick on the ground, and she did something for which nowadays she would have picked up the George Medal. Even in those remote days paper sellers were beginning to be regarded as a special breed, a race apart.

The lady in Renfield Street could be that Paper Nellie. The red tammy has long since gone to a jumble sale and the bare feet are now comfortably and warmly shod. The red cheeks are the colour they were in that almost forgotten colour plate; and her smile holds no hard feelings for the moustache we once drew on it.

"All the news that's fit to print" is the boast of a great American newspaper; but that, as a steady diet, may be just too rich for most of us. The complexities of international politics or the overheated antics of celebrities sometimes seem to us to be taking place in some cloud-cuckoo-land on the other side of the moon. Much more interesting sometimes to hear about that big daft girl in the fruit shop round the corner, remember her? Well, she picked up a first dividend on the pools at the weekend and this morning she appeared for work as usual, picked up a bunch of bananas and stuck them, one at a time, in the manageress's earhole.

Now it can be told. The lady in the royal blue rainwear is not a news lady at all. We can now reveal that she is really Lydia Raskolnikova, a colonel in the KGB. She is on record – and on microfilm – as having run a phoney newspaper stand just this side of the Berlin Wall and earlier near the Great Wall of China. Both of these were known information drops. Once she tried to kill James Bond with a poisoned headline.

The gentleman has just made contact with her. The fifty pence piece he handed over for his newspaper was covered with microdots. He was obviously an amateur, giving the game away by not waiting for change. The crocuses in the foreground are really special cathode ray tubes and microphones. Eat your heart out, John Le Carré.

A new and unsullied hoarding seems to have the same irresistible attraction for people with something, or someone, to advertise as a new fall of snow has for children. This one, in Anderston, defines the site on which will eventually grow the new Holiday Inn. By some tacit territorial agreement (who orders these things?) this section of the hoarding seems to have been allocated to pop music and show business. The posters, regimented side by side, assume the aspect of a gigantic stamp album. The policeman takes it all in his stride. He didn't get to be a sergeant hanging around studying coloured pictures of Billy Connolly and Lena Martell.

Once upon a time, in the days when producers and consumers had a face-to-face relationship, Glasgow was a city of markets. There were markets for fruit, fish, meat, even a bird market. The mass influx, in the eighteen forties, of the impoverished Irish brought yet another market into being, this one dealing in old clothes. For obvious reasons it became known as "Paddy's Market". In 1875 it went indoors for the first time when the old Bridgegate was being drastically redeveloped and remained in the Old Clothes Hall until that building was demolished in 1922. "Paddy's Market" then reverted to the lanes it had emerged from almost fifty years earlier and where it still flourishes. These days it affords the ironical spectacle of middle-class trendies rummaging among the cast-offs of the working class. Diversification, too, would seem to be the order of the day.

Since the end of World War Two, hair has become something more than the stuff that grows on the top of our heads. It has become a means of self-expression; a badge of the unconventional; a weapon in the perpetual war between the generations. Buttressed by the appropriate epithet, it can become a term of abuse. It has even been the subject of an eponymous and very successful musical. Glasgow is not short of avant-garde hairdressers who will realize, on request, styles that apparently spring from the fantasies of a mad topiarist; yet, at the same time, the more traditional barber shops manage to co-exist: places dedicated to the basic tonsorial precept that the only way to cut hair is – off.

Perhaps it is the association with an old poem about a wee cooper of Fife that deluded us into imagining that the making of barrels was a lost art which vanished into limbo with the magnificent Clydesdale horses that used to pull the fearsomely laden drays of captive hogsheads. We may also have been misled by lorries delivering horrid shiny kegs that look like alcoholic Daleks; and by the fact that poor students no longer tramp two hundred miles to universities, carrying a bag of oatmeal and a barrel of salt herrings. Any modern Guy Fawkes, disillusioned by the two-party system, will be glad to know that a firm in Brand Street, Govan, can still supply him with barrels for his gunpowder.

Nostalgics will remember the scrap
merchant, the ragman whose scooping
call was one of the most colourful of the
old Glasgow street cries. Occasionally it
might be substituted by a raucous blast on
a battered bugle. The ragman offered, in
return for rags, paper windmills which
seemed to be fitted with an instant
self-destruct mechanism or balloons that
proved to be equally short-lived. On very
rare occasions the transactions involved
cash. Formerly one of the low men on the
social totem pole, the ragman nowadays is
up there with the advanced thinkers.
Whether he knows it or not, he is, to quote
the current jargon, "into recycling".

This building that faces on to Glasgow Green dates back to the year of the Indian Mutiny, and is a disused carpet factory. It belonged to James Templeton who had graduated from Paisley shawls to the manufacture of chenille carpets. Wanting to build a factory on Glasgow Green, he was told by the City Fathers of the day that buildings facing on to it should present a pleasing appearance. So he called in William Leiper, a shy, retiring bachelor from Helensburgh.

Now shy, retiring bachelors from Helensburgh (or indeed from anywhere) are strange, cryptic people behind whose bashful exteriors may lurk a criminal or a crusader. And it was known that Leiper had at one time abandoned architecture in favour of painting. Ignoring all this, James Templeton called William Leiper to his office and asked him what he considered to be the most beautiful building in the world. "The Doge's Palace in Venice" said the shy, retiring bachelor from Helensburgh, and was forthwith instructed to draw up plans for a replica, which were accepted. Work then went ahead without further incident, if you except the time a gable wall collapsed and killed twenty-nine women.

Essentially the building has become a memorial to a shy, retiring bachelor who lived all his life in Helensburgh and whose only other known vice was a passion for cycling. It is interesting to speculate what might have happened had his favourite building been the Taj Mahal or, worse, Edinburgh Castle.

Firms that market paint have their own mercantile poetry. Colours that the trade categorize under unromantic British standard numbers undergo a Cinderella transformation on shade cards, with names like Hibiscus, Dolly Grey, and Oxford Blue. Sometimes the names change while the shade remains constant. Thus last year's Dental Pink becomes this season's Debutante. Sometimes the given name has not the remotest affinity with the colour it allegedly describes. There seems, therefore, no reason for not having a tint called Glasgow Green that would recall for expatriates the mercury hue of the Clyde and the magnificent ironwork tracery of the Saracen fountain which seems to owe more to a crochet hook than to a blast furnace.

The girl at the Barrows had her mother worried. "See her! Head's full o' horses". We suggested that this is a phase all young girls have to go through. "Doesn't get it from my side o' the family", the mother said. The influence of television perhaps? "You could be right there. Glued to the box, she is, when that showjumpin' is on. Pictures o' Princess Anne in her bedroom and here's me voted Labour all my days. Dead embarrassin'." What about boyfriends? "Not interested. Boys have only two legs." What about her father then? Perhaps he had influenced her? "No way. He knows nothin' about horses. He'll tell you that himself when he comes back from the bettin' shop."

Ma granny says her mammy
(her name wis same as mine)
came here frae County Donegal
in eighteen-fifty-nine.

Ma mammy says her granny
(she brought up fourteen weans)
wis deid an' buried long afore
they first made airyplanes.

Ma granny says her mammy
had never went tae school
(on winter mornings when it's wet
Ah think she wis nae fool).

The saddest thing they tell me
(it gey near maks me greet)
when she came here – nae hooses,
nae hooses 'n nae street.

Ma mammy says her granny
looked oot at grass a' day:
Nae hooses 'n nae street – Ah mean,
where did she go tae play?

Part of the treason of the twentieth-century intellectual has been the steady attempt to undermine youth organizations like the Boy Scouts and the Boys' Brigade. Intellectuals of both Left and Right have combined in their denigration, despite the fact that both Hitler and Stalin flattered by imitation. The Scouts are, possibly, the more international in outlook and, paradoxically, more English. It is still besieged, one feels, inside Mafeking, and its ethos is still pre-industrial. The Boys' Brigade, perhaps because it was founded in Glasgow, has always been stubbornly urban. Ask down any street where a boy is learning to play the bugle in the BB band.

THE BOYS' BRIGADE
WAS FOUNDED HERE BY
WILLIAM ALEXANDER SMITH
ON THE FOURTH DAY OF
OCTOBER 1883 AND THE
ORIGINAL COMPANY OPERATED
HERE FOR NINETY YEARS

Mal commune, mezzo gaudio, says an Italian proverb; an evil shared is half a joy. The words should have been raised above the entrance to every public wash-house in Glasgow. The "steamie", as it was popularly called, took the necessary evil of washing day and changed it into an affirmation of community. The steamie was where you went to catch up with the local news and gossip and to contribute your own small quota. The modern laundrette is a place of alienation catering for transients, singletons and loners. And even the most advanced home washing machine is singularly uncommunicative about the goings-on of that problem family that lives in Number Twenty-seven.

· NOTICE ·
ANY PERSON WHO INTERFERES WITH the COMFORT of OTHERS in the WASH-HOUSE OR USES PROFANE, INDECENT or OFFENSIVE LANGUAGE Will be TURNED OUT of the PREMISES and not PERMITTED to RETURN.

Glasgow has succeeded in projecting a world-wide image of itself as a great bastion of *machismo*. The sad thing is that intellectuals, Glasgow intellectuals, who should know better, have also accepted this image. Of all the commentators on the city only its cartoonists have told the truth. Glasgow has a long and honourable line of them, the greatest being the late Bud Neill. The speed at which they must work and their reliance on topicality save them from the distortions of theory. They leave hindsight to psychiatrists and tell it like it is. And what emerges is that Glasgow is a matriarchy. The waitresses taking a break in a well-known coffee house are amused that anyone should ever have thought otherwise.

Glasgow's coffee houses, we are convinced, came into existence as a means of circumventing the Protestant Work Ethic. The city's businessmen arrive at the office, open the mail and repair immediately to the coffee house where they spend the rest of the morning – and sometimes part of the afternoon – safely insulated from the shocks of commerce. Apologists for this way of life will tell you that a great deal of business is actually transacted in Glasgow's coffee houses; but years of dedicated eavesdropping have only brought us volumes of tedious information about golf handicaps, Dragon Class yachts, and the piratical practices of garage mechanics.

It is surprising that Glasgow's architects whose versatility embraced public buildings, warehouses and even coffee shops should never have turned their attention to designing pubs. The likelihood is that people like Mackintosh and "Greek" Thomson were never asked to do so. Publicans may have worried that their customers would be so carried away by some exquisite detail of Mackintoshery that they would forget the reason for being in a pub at all. One senses an opportunity lost. In view of his strictures on Glasgow's philistinism plus his known love of a dram, Mackintosh might have preferred to be remembered for a pub building rather than for the Glasgow School of Art.

The camera never lies. It is just that reality itself sometimes disguises itself in the trappings of fantasy. The lighting in the Griffin Bar, on the corner of Elmbank Street and Bath Street, creates a scene from a film about the Blitz; or it could be a sequence from some scary doomwatch epic about those perpetual hostiles that lurk in the depths of space. The tiny amber man from Planet Toink observes the results of his laser beam attack. When the lights change the Red Clone will take over with the Green Clone there or thereabouts. Meanwhile, the two earthlings keep their cool. Dr Who has successfully handled worse situations than this.

The Victorian mediaeval revival failed to make as powerful an impact on pragmatic Glasgow as it did south of the border. This is puzzling since, if we regard this phenomenon as a reaction to the materialistic horrors of the Industrial Revolution, the West of Scotland had more than ample justification for being part of it. Nevertheless, Glasgow studios produced superb stained glass, perhaps to show the world that anything London could do Glasgow could do better. An incomprehensible prejudice against stained glass has resulted in much of their work being destroyed; but the names of Stephen Adam, Daniel Cottier and Harrington Mann deserve to be better known.

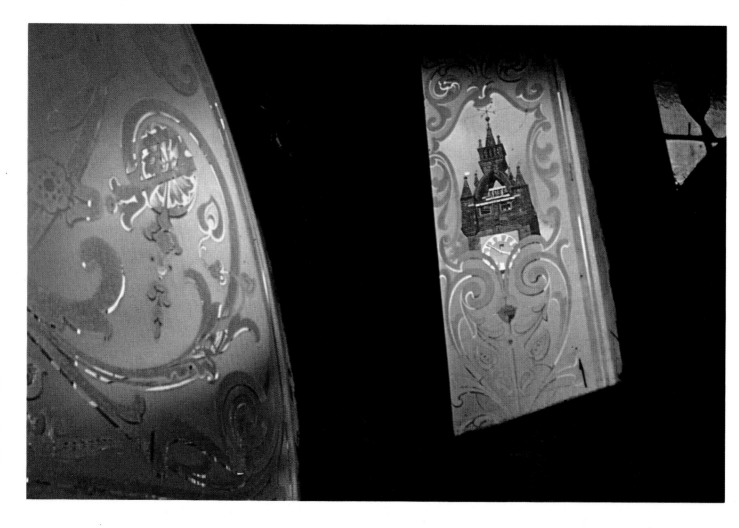

The Tolbooth steeple which dates back to
1626 is seen here by the twentieth-century
eye. From 1736 onwards, the citizens
could tell what day it was by listening to
the musical bells from the steeple. On
Sundays, they played "Easter Hymn".
Monday brought "Gilderoy". "Nancy's tae
the Greenwood gane" meant it was
Tuesday while Wednesday's signature
tune was "Tweedside". That delightful air
"The Lass o' Patie's Mill" identified
Thursday. Friday had a certain
end-of-the-week finality with "The Last
Time I Cam' O'er The Muir". Saturday was
"Roslin Castle". What happened if you
were tone-deaf remains shrouded in
mystery.

Glasgow buildings are decorated with astonishing details, some of which are more comic than tasteful by contemporary standards. The cherubs defying wind and weather in St Vincent Street have been explaining to each other for years why they never made it as jockeys. On the other side of the river, the blinded figure is thankful not to be able to see how motorists drive on the Kingston Bridge. High above Clyde Street on the old Fish Market, Pegasus is alert and at the service of any merchant who has to pursue escaping flying fish. The earthbound semi-halo warns patrons of a swimming pool that they just can't walk on water any old how.

First the shipbuilders proved that iron ships could float, and that led the architects to get into the act. This warehouse in Jamaica Street was designed by John Baird and is a perfect combination of iron and stone. It floats above the street as light and graceful as a clipper ship and every bit as functional.

The Royal Automobile Club on the east side of Blythswood Square was originally designed as a block of private houses. Built in 1823, the architect was John Brash. The building belies his name, being rather staid, as were probably the well-to-do occupiers. As soon as we said that, we remembered Madeleine Smith who lived just around the corner.

The inspiration perhaps for that Judy Garland song, "The place above the chimney tops where troubles melt like lemon drops"? Unimaginative fact says it is the roof of the Merchants' House at the corner of Queen Street and George Street. The chimney pots face each other in some weirdly egalitarian chess game in which kings, queens, knights, bishops and pawns have all been reduced to a common denominator. The Merchant Guilds' ship on top of the dome catches the sun and, looking west we see the steeple of St George's Tron as it raises stone arms in horror at the galloping democracy of the washing on the line.

The shank of the evening in Great Western Road: too late to go to the theatre or the cinema, too early yet to go home. The last dying rays of the sun turn a tower block into a parody of melt-down. Nearer the camera, two older buildings, both of them churches, fade modestly into silhouette. The one farthest away is St Mary's Episcopal Cathedral, the nearer one is Landsdowne United Presbyterian Church. Built in 1862, its slender steeple uncannily previews the shape of Mach Three aircraft to come. In 1862, it was greeted by an anonymous couplet: "This church was no built for the poor and needy, but for the rich and Doctor Eadie."

The Reverend Doctor Eadie remained singularly unmoved.

This is where you take an expatriate Glaswegian who emigrated at the end of World War Two and is now revisiting his native city for the first time since then. When he has been stunned by the total disappearance of Castle Street, you stop mercifully here. "Isn't this where the Garngad was?" he asks tentatively, or "Is that the convent still up there on the top of the hill?" The next question comes from a policeman who wants to know what you're doing parked in the middle of the motorway.

An image may sometimes persist when the actuality has faded and gone, the Cheshire Cat's grin being the classic example. Even today the word "Gorbals" conjures up squalor, violence and deprivation. Yet the bad old Gorbals, now vanished, had its own reasons for pride: Benny Lynch, Scotland's first ever world boxing champion; more famous footballers then you could show a red card to; the internationally acclaimed Citizens Theatre. A Gorbals MP, Andrew Bonar Law, became British Prime Minister. It is also claimed that Gorbals contains the only housing scheme in Britain to be built without a single windowpane being broken.

It may be that like certain wines they do not travel well. Skyscrapers which function successfully in other countries acquire a sour taste here and a bad press to match. One eminent architect who used to litter landscapes with them has publicly recanted. They have been pilloried as filing cabinets for people and streets in the sky. Is the truth perhaps that Glaswegians are just not vertical people?

It was that George Formby song that attracted him into the business, which is why he now goes around buying up old 78 rpm records of "When I'm Cleaning Windows" and smashing them. In fifteen years he has seen nothing that would bring a blush to a maiden aunt's cheek. He works alone now since the day his artistic partner got carried away and stepped back to admire his work.

There are plenty of jargon words to describe the process. You pays your money and you takes your choice. There is "rehabilitation", for example, which has a clinical, off-putting aura about it which we find unsympathetic and uninvolved. Then there is "gentrifying" which is endearingly snobbish and redolent of upward mobility. You can settle for the straightforward, no-nonsense "restoration" if you don't mind inescapable associations with Charles II which, if you are truly upwardly mobile, you won't. Anyway, it all boils down to the same thing – cleaning up old buildings. This process is satisfying, quick, and – of paramount importance these days – cheap. The buildings pictured are in Broomhill Drive.

81

There is a certain received wisdom to the effect that Victorian Glasgow was, like Gath or Askelon, a city of the Philistines. Where are its plays, its novels, its paintings? demands this conventional wisdom and sits back in unassailable smugness. Custodians of this attitude would no doubt be properly shocked to be accused of rigging the ballot, yet essentially this is what they are doing. Art is what we say it is, they declare, and anything else is either not an art form or is an inferior form of art and consequently disenfranchised. It is hard to convince such people that the creative dynamic of nineteenth-century Glasgow may have chosen to express itself in architecture.

Great Western Terrace, built in 1869,

was the work of Alexander Thomson, the most famous architect of them all. He was known as "Greek" Thomson for reasons the picture makes sufficiently obvious. He seems to have been a quiet stay-at-home Victorian behind whose buttoned-up façade there seethed a kind of stylistic corsair who plundered the past for the greater glory of the present. If this was a species of colonialism it made him very much a man of his time, an age when the sun whirled round the British Empire, looking vainly for a place to set.

Thomson was no innovator, yet he had a magic ability to take an old view of things and transform it into a new vision. Someone once described one of his creations as "more Thomson than Greek".

If this was a gibe, it becomes one of those gibes that is really a reluctant tribute. He seems constantly to be headed on a collision course towards vulgarity, but the impact never takes place. He was Cecil B. De Mille with taste. From the terrace he built, Thomson would not have seen a man hurrying home to the warmth, but rather an Athenian soldier bearing news of a battle and, without knowing it, fathering a brand-new Olympic contest.

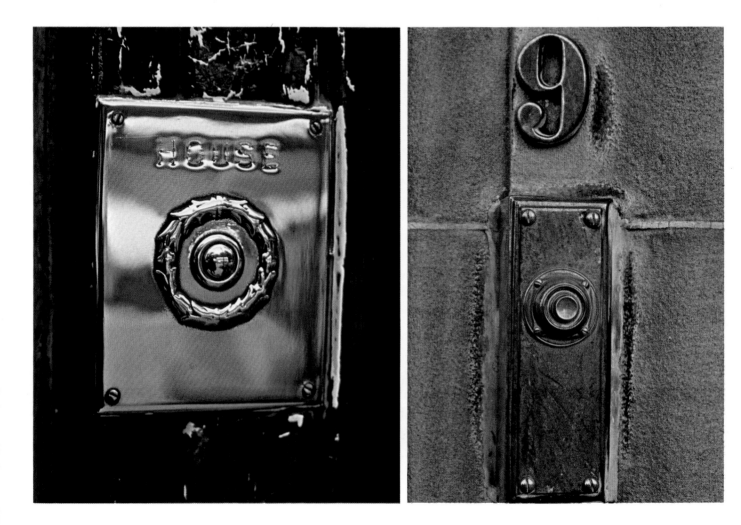

A combination of sounding brass and tinkling cymbal: you press the brass button and somewhere in the inside depths the cymbal tinkles. The door is then opened by a formidable dragon who has been in the family for generations and fears neither God nor man. Or perhaps by a dimpled handmaiden with not a hair out of place and a sexy line in curtseys. That was the scenario then. Nowadays you are inspected through a peephole, checked out by a closed-circuit TV, your motives and intentions X-rayed by a machine. As the H. G. Wells' character observed, "This here progress; it keeps on".

The Sunday word is "fenestration". Weekday people like ourselves simply say "windows". One question that has engaged our spare thoughts over the years is whether the fenestration tells you about the architects who designed the houses or the people who eventually inhabit them. The rectangular windows are severe, presbyterian. Even the lace-edged blinds and the stained glass seem grudging concessions. The soft arch of the other window bespeaks gentler things. The lupins stand like footlights. The curtain is about to go up. It can't possibly be an accident that the window is in Garnethill, once a famous area for theatrical digs.

85

Two Glasgow solutions to the problem of dealing with the world outside. The first seems to act on the principle of using the external bleakness to accentuate the internal cosiness. The second blanks it out entirely, to interpose between you and it a new world of fantasy. And fantasy provokes a strange thought. Did Walt Disney ever sojourn in Glasgow? If so, was some seed planted in his unconscious mind to flower triumphantly later? Before you dismiss the speculation out of hand, look steadily at the stained glass for two minutes. Eventually you will see Donald Duck.

Glasgow diet is the despair of dieticians everywhere. Not only is it bad, they say, it is wilfully bad. This group of Garnethill schoolgirls is doing its best to drive their dietician into early retirement or a job in a factory manufacturing dental plastic. They are perhaps at an age when mathematics does not include the counting of calories, when they have digestions like ostriches which can cope with iron nails. They pay no more attention to those who would save them from themselves than they do to the gable-end art in the background.

The subtleties of class distinction and social snobbery are at once infinite and local. Speech, dress, hairstyles – all carry the added meanings of who you are and where you stand on the social ladder. Every city has its good addresses and its socially no-go areas. In Glasgow, for example, to live up a wally close was an unspoken statement of your credit rating, of your accent, the schools your children attended or would attend in due course, the kind of clubs you joined or that would be prepared to have you as a member. All this information was coded in the fact that the entrance to where you lived had half-tiled walls.

The scent of musk, we recall reading somewhere, once vanished overnight. The same thing could almost be said about the Glasgow potteries. Indeed, the year 1933 could be credibly assigned as the date of the disappearance. Up until then there were potteries all over the city, and their mergers and break-ups, partnerships and rivalries, failures and successes, family feuds and dynastic marriages have become a fascinating field for the specialist student. Glasgow pottery is now very much in, and such names as Bell, Cochrane, Lockhart, Balfour or Fleming on an item are guaranteed to make dealers drool and collectors get itchy chequebooks. The beautiful piece shown is in the People's Palace.

89

Kate Cranston was a remarkable lady. A member of a long-established hotel-owning Glasgow family, with an equally remarkable eye for an architect. She also had a much rarer quality, an ability not to insist on calling the tune just because she was paying the piper. When in 1903 she commissioned Charles Rennie Mackintosh to design a tea room for her she gave him a free hand. The result was something unique in interior decoration. With a little help from his wife – an artist in her own right – Mackintosh designed every aspect of the tea room, right down to the teaspoons. Soon the Willow Tearoom at 217 Sauchiehall Street was the smart place to go. Now it has been lovingly restored.

So much has been written and talked about Charles Rennie Mackintosh in recent years that he is in danger of becoming a bore. The simple remedy, however, is to go and look at the original. Mackintosh was a functionalist. His dictum was simple: if it doesn't function, forget it. The Library in his Glasgow School of Art shows the precept in practice. It is light, lean, spare. Any statements it makes are made without verbiage. But Glasgow seemed to prefer rhetoric, and Mackintosh gave up. He is still a much more widely respected figure on the Continent where he ended his days, drinking, railing at Glasgow, and painting remarkable watercolours.

Since the heady militant days of 1968
student power has changed from a
middle-class bogey into a more easily
tolerable form of wild oats. If truth be told,
the Glasgow student, even at Mackintosh's
School of Art, has always been a creature
of unrewarding cosiness. The wild
undergraduate, torn between booze and
books, philosophy and fun, perhaps only
ever existed in the memories of
middle-aged alumni. When dramatist
James Bridie describes the student of his
day as "lively, violent, unprejudiced,
friendly, noisy, sympathetic, moderate
even in riot, interested, disinterested,
intelligent, balanced, unaffected, chaste,
adaptable, etcetera", one suspects that he
was being paid by the word.

Van Gogh never went to art school nor did
Gauguin. Grandma Moses never had a
lesson in her life. Talent is the thing every
time, and you can't teach talent, can you?
The argument for and against art schools
is perpetual. When a decision was arrived
at not so very long ago to require a certain
level of academic achievement from
students entering art school, we pursed
our lips and shook our heads, thinking of
unlettered shepherd boys of blazing
brilliance barred from their birthright.
Until such a phenomenon appears on our
doorstop, we're pro art schools as places
that reassure mum and dad that wanting to
be a painter is not something that should
be treated by men in white coats.

Charles Rennie Mackintosh's approach to designing houses was simple, indeed unilateral. When he said he would design a house for you, he meant it in a total kind of way. Everything inside and out was pure Mackintosh. If you were unmarried he would design a wife for you, plus two and a quarter assorted children if the interior decoration called for that. The ladderback chair was probably designed for a house with a butler six metres tall. Or it may have been a place of refuge if the lady of the house was confronted by a maddened mouse. It would be handy when the ceiling needed painting. And it is even possible that Charles Rennie M. was sending us all up.

Most of us are content with one solitary signature. Mackintosh had dozens, all, in some strange way, peculiar to him, valid, and instantly recognizable. Details on a battered door announce the master. His style of lettering can be imitated but recalls Mackintosh and not the imitator. He is impossible to plagiarize. One is uneasily aware of a possibly darker side to the great architect. He plays tricks with conventional geometric shapes. His stained-glass figure is emerging from a black hole. It could be some type of mutant, a giant cicada. It has a weird frontal bone, shaped and finned like a missile. It zeroes in on similar strange creatures in the dark recesses of the human mind.

Farewell, midnight oil. And lecturers with cleft palates and books that made so little sense to the brain you had to learn them by heart, and stomach-churning waiting for the pass lists in *The Glasgow Herald*. Gone, all gone.

His hangover from last night's party amost gone too. Mum takes a picture of Alastair and Dad. Didn't he look handsome as he went up for his scroll? And cool. The kids nowadays . . . . She photographs from an upright stance as though standing to attention out of respect to the day, to Alastair, to the place, to everything. And the rain stayed off too.

Dad smiles at the camera. Now his son has a degree, something he never got. He is suddenly aware that his son is bigger than he is. A fugitive flicker of unease lights up his mind. He exorcises it by taking on the role of cameraman.

Alastair and Dad – Alastair's graduation. Alastair on his graduation day. Alastair and Mum – Alastair's graduation. The second time Dad achieves a real laid-back style. Tonight champagne.

Mum, her shoes slipped off beneath the table, talks to the maître d'.

"My son graduated today."

"I'm so happy for you, madam."

"He's going to help me order the meal in French."

"Oui, madame."

"Alastair, what's the French for crêpe suzette?"

It is no exaggeration to state that if
Glasgow University, whose tower is seen
here lurking behind the trees, had been a
play it would have been taken off after a
week's run. After four hundred and
fourteen years of academic squalor in the
High Street, the University Senate
appointed Sir G. Gilbert Scott to build a
new home for them in Gilmorehill. Sir
Gilbert's building received universally
hostile reviews. In 1866 the first sod was
cut. Two years later, the Prince and
Princess of Wales came up to lay the
foundation stone. He was made a freeman
of the city. He was honoured with an LL.D.
He knighted the Lord Provost. He caused
the city to be gaily illuminated. But he
couldn't make professional architects like
the building. They still don't.

The pomp and circumstance are at an end. The custodians can relax into human attitudes. The judge descends, or even condescends, to less harsh areas of judgment, passing less far-reaching verdicts on a glass of port or a twenty-year-old malt whisky. Perhaps in today's new crop of graduates he has seen his own continuance, some bright young man – perhaps even some bright young woman – destined to bring new concepts, new insights, new methods, even new mercies to the eternal problem of dealing with human beings and their vagaries: some future pioneer in the complexities of intergalactic legalities or computer law. We feed into the pictured conversation heavy profundities that might not be justified if we heard the actual words played back on tape. Time has its own overpowering authority which is buttressed by the medievalism of the costumes and the ceremony. Even Glasgow's determined, and sometimes depressing, egalitarianism is temporarily in abeyance. Who would seriously maintain that a parchment awarded by a gowned figure amid cadenzas of Latin is the same as one handed over by a resolute democrat in a boiler suit?

A conversation piece in the Groves of Academe. What do they talk about there? What do the recipients of honorary degrees say to the entrenched academics? Is the chat high-powered, sprinkled with quotations from Spinoza, Hegel and Kierkegaard, lightened by flashes of donnish wit? Lively wordplay in dead languages. Or is it low-key, sprinkled with quotations from the Financial Times Share Index, lightened by promises of grants to come from industrial tycoons. Do the proceedings grind slowly to a solemn halt or does the punch flow like water with everyone ending up throwing bread rolls and Ph.D.s at each other?

There is no such thing as an unmixed blessing. The starving Irish who poured into Glasgow during the famine years of the nineteenth century brought with them, as well as their undoubted qualities of wit, gaiety, courage and endurance, the sectarian bitterness which, depressingly, sometimes seems to constitute the whole of Irish history. There is an intolerance in Glasgow that co-exists surprisingly with its reputation as a friendly city. There is a mythical story of a newcomer being quizzed as to his religious affiliations. No, he wasn't a Catholic. No, he wasn't a Protestant either. Whereupon both sides beat him up for being an atheist.

The Voice of the People is the Voice of God. It is only right, then, that when the will of the people has been expressed in choosing its elected representatives, the victors of the ballot box should be solemnly presented in the house of God for His approval. This ceremony takes place in Glasgow Cathedral and is known as the Kirking of the Council. A black Glasgow rumour that the Cathedral will fall down the day an honest man forms part of the procession may be discounted as a sour-grapes invention by a group of failed candidates.

A cenotaph, the dictionary says, is an empty tomb, a monument raised to someone buried elsewhere. Here, in Glasgow, on the Day of Remembrance, a man's expression suggests that a man's memory may be the best cenotaph of all, that it may contain within itself the names of those who died in the desert, who perished in brewed-up tanks, who lay face down in the uncaring hot sand and were not warmed by the hot sun of Libya. He stands in the Glasgow rain at the eleventh hour of the eleventh day of the eleventh month, wondering what happened to the bullet that had his name on it, wondering who decides this one should live and that one die, wondering and mourning.

The ideal secret society, of course, should never bring into existence any mention or trace of itself; but this is perhaps too much to demand of human beings. So secret societies invent grips, passwords and other techniques of mutual identification. We must confess, however, that we had never regarded a stained glass window as one of these. Language, too, can sometimes paradoxically be a mechanism of secrecy, and highly satisfying it must be to talk quite openly in front of the enemy without him being any the wiser.

The City of Glasgow has the second highest number of Gaelic speakers in Scotland.

The early years of the last century were bonanza time for the body-snatching business in Glasgow. Graveyards all over the city were raided, and the bodies dug up were smuggled to the dissection tables of the College. When a ship from Ireland berthed at the Broomielaw and started to unload what were allegedly bags of rags, it was soon discovered that the rags were actually human cadavers. During the ensuing outcry, the Magistrates issued edicts calling on citizens to patrol the burial grounds. High railings were erected around individual graves, and foiling the resurrectionists almost became Glasgow's favourite sport. Among the devices used for the purpose was the mortsafe, basically a heavy stone embedded on top of the tomb. This one is in the Cathedral burial ground.

This church, the Wellington United Presbyterian Church in University Avenue, recalls the story of the wealthy tycoon who claimed to have, preserved in its original condition, the hammer with which his great-grandfather had started the original business. When pressed, he would admit that, during the years, it had had seventeen new heads and that the shaft had been replaced even more often, but so what? It was the hammer with which his great-grandfather, etcetera, etcetera. The church pictured began as the Relief Church in Cheapside Street in Anderston. That was in 1770. The congregation moved to Wellington Street and a new building in 1827. This building had "sepulchral vaults" which were entered from West Campbell Street. The final move to University Avenue sent the ancient bones to "the Necropolis and elsewhere", which sounds as though the bones were given some sort of choice. Or maybe it was to prevent them rattling in Calvinistic fury at being buried beneath a Greek temple.

If we were given our choice of where to live in Glasgow it would have to be on Woodlands Hill, overlooking the twelve acres of Kelvingrove Park. Once called the West End Park, it was laid out by Charles Wilson and Joseph Paxton for the recreation of the increasingly affluent citizens of the West End. Wilson must have fallen in love with the situation for, in the late 1850s he designed Park Circus, thus providing the nucleus of what has been described in the definitive work on Glasgow architecture as "the most striking piece of town design in Glasgow". The view from the hilltop is superb, and on a clear day, the story goes, you can see the last mortgage payment. Most of the houses are now occupied as business premises, which tells you a lot about present-day priorities. Another thing we have never been able to understand is what exactly Lord Roberts V.C. is doing sitting up there on his charger. Did he ever dream during his famous march from Kabul to Kandahar that he would end up overseeing one of the most beautiful blocks of buildings in Glasgow?

There is more to the stony, bearded gentleman who broods on one end of the bridge on Kelvin Way than meets the eye. Originally he was Number Three of a group of four and at the time – May 1914 – that the project got the green light from the Corporation, he was meant to represent either Progress or Prosperity. In 1917 when the sculptor exhibited full-size models at the Royal Academy, he had become either Philosophy or Inspiration which may have been sculptor Paul Montford's wry comment on the foundry receiving fifteen hundred pounds more than he did. Blown into the river in 1941, Philosophy/Inspiration remained there for nine years before being fished out, badly damaged and with several parts missing, to be bionically restored by Glasgow sculptor, Benno Schotz.

The final balance sheet of the first
International Exhibition of Science and
Art, held in Glasgow between May and
November 1888, showed a healthy
surplus of over fifty-four thousand
pounds. Forty-six thousand of this was
immediately set aside for the laudable
purpose of building an Art Gallery and
Museum "worthy of the name and
enterprise of the City". Everybody started
to get into the act. Sir John Muir came up
with fifteen thousand. A few prominent
citizens contributed four times that
amount plus a free site in Kelvingrove
Park. Whereupon the Corporation added
a sum equal to the Exhibition surplus. It
all reads like a civic fairy tale nowadays.
The photograph shows the main hall.

A small child in the Armour Room of the Museum discovers that long before Star Wars there were War Stars; and their latter-day reincarnations such as Darth Vader probably have the ironic effect of enabling him to relate more easily to the medieval mementoes than he can to the tramcars in the Glasgow Transport Museum. This seems a pity for the Glasgow "caur" is, and should continue to be, part of the city's folklore. In its heyday, the Glasgow tramway system was the cheapest and most efficient form of public transport in the world. Its successive supremos were neither of them local men. Perhaps there is a moral here: Glasgow transport is too important to be run by Glaswegians.

Glaswegians queue up in Kelvingrove
Park to prove yet once again that the
Glasgow punter has the worst teeth and
the sweetest tooth in the country. Sweets
and sugary soft drinks are consumed each
year in mind-boggling quantities. The
ruinous dental effects of this orgiastic
indulgence are compounded by the
softness of the drinking water whose
potability we personally have found
unmatched anywhere. The fountain in the
background left is the Stewart Memorial
Fountain commemorating the Lord
Provost who masterminded the laying-on
of the delectable water supply. It comes
from three lochs; Loch Katrine, Loch
Venachar, and – make of this what you will
– Loch Drunkie.

Three miles from the city centre, in 360 acres of its own grounds, stands Pollok House, an Adam building, built in 1747 for Sir John Maxwell. In 1966 it was presented to the National Trust for Scotland and to Glasgow Corporation, along with the Stirling-Maxwell collection of furniture, porcelain, silver, glass and paintings. For years the Corporation had been embarrassed by the problem of a different windfall, the Burrell Bequest, an immense accumulation of artefacts of all ages, picked up all over the world by a wealthy shipping magnate with a jackdaw's acquisitiveness and the means to indulge it. Now a Burrell Museum is being built in the grounds of Pollok House.

Sometimes the eccentricities of the Victorian plutocracy appear to us of a more straitened era as weird and wonderful as anything likely to be encountered in the depths of space. The glass buildings above were once the Winter Garden of Mr John Kibble and, no doubt, provided exotic and out-of-season delights for his guests at Coulport on Loch Long. Actually, a visiting Martian could hardly choose a better spot to land. The Botanic Gardens, of which the Kibble Palace is a part, could hardly be improved on as a place to study representative Glaswegians – especially on a fine Sunday morning.

The Botanic Gardens originally occupied some six acres in what was then called Sauchiehall Road. The University had invested two thousand pounds in the venture and this holding entitled the Professor of Botany and his students to free use of the Gardens for purposes of study. The expanding city pushed the Gardens west, and 1842 saw them transplanted to their present site in Kelvinside. Mr Kibble's Palace arrived in 1871 to be re-erected on an enlarged scale. On 5th December 1879, William Ewart Gladstone was installed as Rector of Glasgow University and gave his rectorial address in the Kibble Palace. His chosen theme was "Self-knowledge" and tastefully avoided any reference to people who live in glass houses.

The startled nymph inside the glass dome
of the Kibble Palace has been the subject
of speculation and comment – most of it
ribald – from generations of Glasgow wits.
A divinity student suggested that she
represented Susannah in the moment of
recognizing that the Elders were just
another bunch of dirty old men. A
misogynist saw her as a sort of Mark One
Women's Libber regretting the impulse
that made her burn her bra. Personally we
see her as a Glasgow equivalent of Lot's
Wife who, ordered not to look back at the
wicked cities of the plain, did so and was
immediately turned into a pillar of
sodium chloride.

Some years ago, a Dutch director made a film called *Holland is a Mirror* which consisted entirely of shots of buildings reflected in Dutch rivers and canals. It was an impressive piece of work but, as might have been expected, slightly lacking in human interest. We thought for a moment that our intrepid photographer was about to embark on a similar project, but this single shot of the weir on the River Kelvin seems to have exhausted his interest in what is, after all, really the belabouring of a gimmick. As the Wicked Queen in *Snow-White* used to remark: "When you've seen one mirror shot, you've seen 'em all".

Simeon Ersatz writes in *The Sunday Waffle:* "One work in particular I found really grabbing. The catalogue lists it as "Still Water and Beer Can" but I prefer to recall it as "Backwater". Essentially it is an excercise in green arranged in thirds. The bold, tortured shapes of nightmarish leaves rise aggressively from the first spatial third against a cleverly nauseating impasto of algae. White daisies float with haphazard cunning against a green that has become darker, more insidious in its sinister possibilities of changing the innocent white statements of the daisies into white lies. The beer can holds the composition together and makes its own statement, an off-centre, open-mouthed scream of alienation and despair."

The parents sit on the park bench like
bookends between whom tomorrow is
already slyly writing its own sequels. The
first incomers are generally conservative,
backward-looking, too intent on securing
the beachhead to have time or inclination
for anything else. The small girl is already
much more into her new culture than her
mother is or possibly ever will be. She is
already on the track that is the resultant of
the culture clash on the way to integration.
She speaks her native language at home
only. In the school playground she shouts
Glasgow with the best of them. She has a
big sister at home who is into punk rock
and wears chains, but only when Father
isn't looking.

The Third Eye Centre in Sauchiehall
Street is where it's all at, avant-gardewise.
Whatever you're into: films, T.M.,
feminism, ecology, jazz, folk, ultra-theatre,
mixed media, it's all at the Third Eye. If it
isn't, mention the fact loudly and it will be
next time you call. There is a vegetarian
restaurant and a bar. There is a bookshop
that is rapidly becoming the most
interesting bookshop in the city. Its two
galleries present the works of
international as well as local painting. Our
all-time favourite exhibition was by a
Rumanian whose chosen medium was
gingerbread. If you found his work didn't
grow on you once you got it home, you
simply covered it with custard and ate it.

A strange place to hold an audition, you may think. But the acoustics in this corner of Glasgow University's Hunterian Art Gallery are possibly excellent. And the man with the hat who seems to be conducting the bare-headed man in a rendition of "If I Was A Rich Man" would perhaps rather be doing that than looking at the sapphic decoration that was passed off as painting by mannish ladies in the twenties and thirties. The dance below is from a performance of Scottish Opera's *Eugene Onegin* at the Theatre Royal.

An accidental cloudburst turns the Citizens' Theatre and its immediate environs into a Rorschach Blot. Rorschach, as every sick schoolboy knows, was a Swiss psychiatrist who evolved a technique of presenting his patients with a perfectly symmetrical ink blot and then asking them to voice their reactions and associations. The Rorschach Blot Test is perhaps as valid a way as any other of assessing a theatre as controversial as the Citizens' Theatre is now. At least it has the illusion of impartiality.

The Citizens' Theatre, initially at least, did not appear to have controversy in its horoscope. Its founders were impeccably middle-class with middle-class aspirations: playright James Bridie and Tom Honeyman, Director of the Art Gallery. Oddly enough, both men were qualified doctors of medicine. In 1945, the Citizens' Theatre took over the old Princess' Theatre in the Gorbals where it

remains to this day. Nationalists slam it for its apparently total lack of interest in contemporary Scottish themes and writers. Its defenders point to its undeniably high European reputation. Critics attack it for the sin of formalism, for being more concerned with theatricality than theatre. The defenders say: so what? The truth probably lies, as truth tends to do, between the two embattled extremes. When the Citizens' Theatre is at its best, it offers a theatrical experience second to none anywhere; but at its worst, the experience becomes that of being forcibly fed with candyfloss.

Sir Henry Wood originated the idea. Sir Malcolm Sargent added his flamboyant personality. Now Glasgow has its own season and its own Last Night of the Proms. Traditionally, this finale is a light-hearted occasion. The music is undemanding, tuneful, classical pop. The native flavour comes from Scots songs and pieces like Malcolm Arnold's *Tam o' Shanter Overture.* There are balloons and a great deal of bonhomie. Blue-haired ladies from up West roar out "Land of Hope and Glory". Sir Alexander Gibson conducts it all *con brio*. The Scottish National Orchestra has a ball. Members of the audience are requested not to throw heavy paper darts on to the platform, and a good time is had by all.

Dante and Beatrice, Antony and Cleopatra,
Heloïse and Abelard, great love affairs all,
but pallid, etiolated relationships when
measured against the great Glasgow
passion for football. In Glasgow, the Huns
support the Bears while the Tims root for
the Bhoys or, to put it less colourfully,
Protestants support Glasgow Rangers
while Catholics support Glasgow Celtic. A
small but indomitably faithful crowd of
eccentrics supports Partick Thistle. Over
any year your Glasgow football fan will
travel thousands of miles, spend
hundreds of pounds and talk millions of
words on what has been described by
someone as "basically a simple game".
This is like saying that the Bible is basically
just a book.

A great day in the football calendar is any day when Rangers play Celtic. On the occasion pictured, the confrontation took place at Hampden Park, the stadium which has hosted so many past local and international triumphs and disasters. There is always a great deal of pious moralizing before, during and after encounters between these two leading Glasgow teams; and the greater the violence the greater the hypocritical response. Yet nothing constructive is ever done about it, which makes one wonder if perhaps Glasgow is secretly proud of this always potentially explosive event in the way that Chicago was of Al Capone and his gang in the Prohibition era.

Even in medieval days, Glasgow seems to have been pro-football. At a time when the game was being legislated against everywhere else as interfering with archery practice, the city magistrates were actively encouraging the game, even going so far as to provide the footballs. The burgh minutes of 1575 reveal that the price of a football in those days was twopence. Of course the game then was not the boring eleven-a-side business we endure nowadays but a full-blooded clash of hundreds against hundreds. Is it possible that football violence is merely a reversion to this and that the real game is being played not on the field but on the terracing?

Glasgow has always been, and still is, a curiously fire-prone city. The Great Glasgow Fire of 17 June 1652 burned down a third of the city and made over a thousand families homeless. John K. McDowall in his *People's History of Glasgow* lists no fewer than twenty-six fires between 1875 and 1898, confining himself to fires where the damage caused exceeded twenty thousand pounds. The Central Fire Station is in Ingram Street and was built in 1899. The dog in the glass case was called Wallace. Misunderstanding the meaning of the term "firedog", Wallace wandered into the Central Fire Station and stayed on as its celebrated mascot until called by the Great Fire Chief In The Sky in 1902.

"Whit are these things doon there, Wullie?"

"Toytown sodgers."

"No' very big, are they, Wullie?"

"Jist the right height for hangin' pictures under beds."

"Fancy uniforms but."

"Remind me o' the Cold Cream Guards."

"Ever see onything like them when you wis in the Army, Wullie?"

"We had a bloke in our mob used tae dress up like that. He wis trying tae work his ticket, he said."

"Did he manage it, Wullie?"

"Don't know. He'd left the unit when I came oot o' the glasshoose."

"Bloke here says these Toytown sodgers is advertisin' the Edinburgh Festival, Wullie."

"Whit! Here in Glasgow?"

"Dead liberty, in't it?"

"Pass ower that pile o' bricks 'n we'll see how they behave under fire."

Straight off the lid of a shortbread tin or perhaps out of a painting by Lady Butler, the pipers stride across the Scotstoun Showground. History would indicate Glasgow as an ironical venue for a Highland Gathering but history enjoys such ironies. When Bonnie Prince Charlie had his Highland Gathering in the city in 1745 it was strictly a non-event. So much so that the Young Pretender was only dissuaded with great difficulty from putting the stiff-necked, unwelcoming town to the torch. Instead, he exacted "contributions" to the extent of ten thousand pounds which the canny citizens later reclaimed from the Hanoverian Government. When Charles Edward went off to the North and Culloden, Glasgow's final contribution was one drunken tailor to his army and Miss Clementina Walkinshaw to his bed.

Anyway, there we were at the Highland
Gathering in the Scotstoun Showground
on a bright, beautiful day straight from the
laundry. No Highland blood compelled
our attendance there, no feeling of clan
loyalty. Our ancestors did not have their
own boat at the Flood and the only time
we ever wore a kilt was many long years
ago when we were camping outside
Inverness and somebody stole our
trousers. The truth is that we happened to
hear about the event on Radio Clyde and it
was a glorious day and so we found
ourselves among the Tartan *mafiosi* and
identifying with the duodecimo drum
major who forgot to polish the backs of his
shoes. Our excuse used to be: "A good
soldier never looks behind".

Two Texans from Clydebank – or Clynder or Clachnacuddin – react differently as somebody's grandfather runs across their field of vision. One turns away before all that septuagenarian vigour shames him into abandoning the pint he has just ferried all the way across the ground from the beer tent. The other watches in simple admiration. The old man keeps his eyes fixed straight ahead, recalling a previous occasion when the sight of a long cool beer caused a total collapse of his moral fibre. The young couple, entangled like a Celtic brooch, evoke the same response wherever they go: "Who wears the pants in that relationship?"

The history of the theatre in Glasgow is practically the history of the Fire Brigade. In 1752, a fanatical mob, urged on by a mad mullah, burned down a small wooden theatre near the Cathedral. In 1780, a theatre on the site of the present Central Station was destroyed by fire, having previously escaped destruction by a similar gang. In 1845, the City Theatre went up in a spectacular blaze after a brief existence of some ten weeks. The year 1863 saw the incineration of the Dunlop Street Theatre, and four years later it was the turn of the Theatre Royal in Cowcaddens. This theatre rose from the ashes and remained fire-proof until 1895 when you'll never guess what happened. Also in Cowcaddens the Grand Theatre flared up in 1917. It was rebuilt, but as a cinema. In the mid-fifties of the present century the Queen's Theatre was cremated. The theatre pictured is the King's Theatre in Bath Street. Glasgow playwrights have often been accused of not writing anything that would set a theatre alight. Now we know why. Intuitively they knew that some arsonist or an act of God would beat them to it before they had even put pen to paper.

The Glasgow theatre-going public has always divided itself strictly along class lines. Those who considered themselves to be up-market tended to identify with London taste, turning out to support touring metropolitan successes. The rough, untutored natives preferred their own concept of drama in their own favoured theatres. This concept was rough, broad and unsophisticated, stylized to a degree, and given to spectacular set pieces whose relevance was not always immediately apparent. Sometimes the players in these demotic theatres would attend a visiting London production, steal the plot and as much of the action and dialogue as they could carry away inside their heads, and then re-create it in their own terms to the great satisfaction of everyone except the original writer.

He may look like John the Baptist but he has his head screwed on. His stage gear has all the quiet restraint of an explosion in a paint shop. His act has been called "blasphemous", "obscene" and "tasteless". Those who accuse him of blasphemy turn out on examination to be closet bigots. The obscenity brigade turn out to have the legs of their pianos chastely covered at home. Those who attack him on the grounds of taste find themselves bogged down, when challenged, in a morass of definition. On the other hand, his friends sometimes do him no favours either. They have compared him with Lenny Bruce a weird comparison to say the least. Bruce found the world and humanity disgusting and that disgust was the dynamic that fuelled his act. Our man finds the same world absurd, not worthy of serious consideration. He is essentially apolitical and suspects all politics as being part of the great universal ridiculous hype. This is perhaps his secret. He has brought up front the language and the attitudes of the low man on the totem pole, brought them there in their pure uncensored rawness. He represents the Glasgow punter as the Glasgow punter sees himself: patter merchant, male chauvinist, fond of a bevvy, capable of surviving anything. Our man has already survived the educational system, sectarianism, the folk clubs and countless chat shows. He may even survive success.

In the days when everyone was forming a group, was in a group, or disbanding a group, there was one called Lulu and the Luvvers. What eventually became of the Luvvers is a matter for those eccentrics who specialize in the minutiae of pop music; what happened to Lulu, otherwise Marie Laurie, is something else. Since she took off on her own, the Glasgow girl has flown high. That she is an international star was brought home to us one night in Amsterdam when our host switched on his TV set and there was Lulu on a programme that was otherwise double Dutch to us. From the beginning she has been shrewd enough to diversify, to work hard at extending her range. Now, instead of finding herself fossilized in a single rut, she can claim to be a singer – in a variety of styles – a fine comedienne and film actress.

If the Pavilion Theatre isn't haunted by the ghost of Lex McLean, then it ought to be. Year after year this raunchy comic, who was to Glasgow what Max Miller once was to London, packed the theatre with plump, middle-aged, working-class ladies, geared up for a night out, pleasantly aglow with small refreshments and equipped with high-decibel screeches to greet each outrageous *double entendre* from a comic who had come up the hard way to become a permanent part of the Glasgow theatrical scene. Now there's a new name topping the bill, the name of Glen Daly, a very much underrated comedian in a city that does not usually make that kind of mistake.

126

Glasgow Fair on Glasgow Green.
Stay-at-home holiday-makers swing high
into the wild blue yonder while thousands
of their fellow Glaswegians fly higher,
faster, farther to the Costa Brava, Malta,
Greece, anywhere they can find sunshine.
The Fair, now eight hundred years old,
had for a long time the same kind of
reputation as Donnybrook Fair. It sobered
up during the last century, the heyday of
the Clyde paddle-steamers and the Clyde
coast holiday resorts. The aeroplane has
changed the pattern again, ferrying the
populace in thousands towards the sun.
Glaswegians love this; for any one of them
will cheerfully admit that the last fortnight
in July – Glasgow Fair Fortnight – is the
wettest two weeks of the year.

Ah'm jist a Glesca wumman,
An ordinary wife,
Nuthin' much has ever happened
Tae me a' ma life.
Ah niver got a prize at school,
Ah niver won a footba' pool,
Ah niver won at bingo no' even by a fluke.
But yin thing Ah'm determined,
Aye, that's the word, determined.
BY HOOK OR BY CROOK
AH'LL BE LAST IN THIS BOOK!